Making & Decorating
FRAMES

FRAMING TECHNIQUES BY
GRAHAM PORTER

MINI · WORKBOOK · SERIES

MEREHURST

CONTENTS

*Découpaged frame with shutters (top left), painted frame (far left)
and decorated frame (left)*

Framing

Picture framing is a rewarding craft, and with the help of this book you will be able to enjoy making your own picture frames at home and have the satisfaction of obtaining professional results—without the cost.

STARTING OUT

If you only make six to eight frames a year, then it is well worth buying some basic framing equipment. You may already have some of the items necessary for framing in your household toolbox.

This cardboard frame is decorated by swirling hot glue over the surface to create a faux embossed appearance.

Good framing begins with colour and design. Colour is the first element that people respond to when they see an object, so selecting the colour of the mount is very important. Generally, lighter colours work best, as dark colours tend to distract the eye from the picture or other object being framed. Similarly, try to select a moulding that is in keeping with the style of artwork being framed. For example, use a blue colour-washed timber frame for a beach scene, or an ornate gold frame for a traditional oil painting.

There is a variety of frame mouldings available, ranging from very ornate styles to plain mouldings which can be painted or decorated as desired. Generally, the idea is to complement and enhance the picture being framed: to create an overall result that draws the viewers' attention in to the picture.

The first half of this book explains how to construct and assemble a basic frame—how to cut glass and mount board—the second half covers a range of techniques used to decorate or revamp your existing wooden frames, ranging from applying a simple coat of paint, to covering frames in fabric. And frames need not be constructed of wood—this book also explains how to make a simple frame from cardboard or papier-mâché.

A visit to a framing shop or art gallery can provide inspiration for your own framing project—look at the style and variety of frames used, the subject being framed and how the mount board is used to enhance the overall effect.

The mount board will greatly enhance the overall look of the frame and artwork. The mount board itself helps lead the eye into the picture by creating a 'breathing space' between the artwork and the frame.

Cutting mount board

The mount is the cardboard window that surrounds the picture. Choosing an appropriate colour for the mount will affect the appearance of the picture even more than the frame itself. The mount not only complements the picture but prevents the artwork being in direct contact with the glass.

EQUIPMENT

- Mount board
- Scrap piece of mount board or heavy card as the slip sheet
- Steel or aluminium ruler
- Tape measure
- Pencil
- Craft knife
- Eraser
- Mount cutter
- Hardboard for backing
- Masking tape

CUTTING THE MOUNT BOARD

1 Decide how much of the picture you want to show through the window of the mount. This is called the 'image size'. Normally you will want to show as much of the image as possible but the mount has to encroach at least 5 mm around the edge of the picture. This is to allow enough room for the picture to move slightly within the frame and not flick through the window.

Thus, if a picture has an overall size of 170 x 255 mm, the image size will be 160 x 245 mm (5 mm is deducted from each side). Then decide on the width of the mount board border. For a border measuring 70 mm on three sides and 85 mm on the bottom, the overall width of the mount board will be as follows:

160 mm + 70 mm + 70 mm = 300 mm

and the overall depth will be:

245 mm + 70 mm + 85 mm = 400 mm.

2 Place the mount board on a large piece of scrap board and mark the overall dimensions in pencil on the reverse side. Mount board usually has 90 degree corners but you may wish to check it using a carpenter's square. Cut out the size and shape required using a metal ruler and craft knife.

CUTTING BLADES
Remember that mount cutter blades are very sharp and should be handled carefully and disposed of thoughtfully. The blade should be replaced after cutting four or five mounts.

CHOOSING MOUNT BOARD COLOURS

When selecting a mount, consider not only the colour but the amount of border you want to be visible. Art supply shops and picture framing suppliers usually have a good supply of mount boards with a range of over eighty colours to choose from. If you are framing a watercolour for example, pick a light colour that matches the overall colour tone of the painting, such as a soft green, pale yellow or ivory. Similarly, a soft brown or beige mount may be suited to an old sepia-toned photograph. Generally, try to avoid bright, vivid colours as these may overpower the artwork.

3 Prepare the mount cutter by adjusting the blade so that it cuts through the mount board and slightly into the slip sheet or spare mount board beneath. (A self-healing cutting mat does not have a firm surface and is not recommended for cutting mount board.)

4 Using a ruler and pencil and working on the back of the mount, mark the borders, measuring in from the outside edge. Marking the borders on the back of the board keeps the front of the mount clean and free of pencil marks. Most mount cutters have a mark near the blade which you can align with the pencil marks for accurate stopping and starting. For the example in step 1, the measurements for the mount are 70 mm from the top and sides and 85 mm from the bottom.

5 Following the instructions on your mount cutter, cut out the window. It is important to slightly overcut in each direction so that the window falls out at the completion of the final cut. If this does not happen, complete the cut using a spare blade or scalpel. The window should fall cleanly away.

ADDING THE BACKING

6 Cut a piece of hardboard to the same overall dimensions as the mount. This serves both as backing board for the whole picture and to hold it in place.

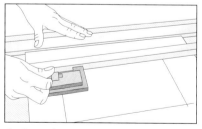

5 Cut the window out with the mount cutter, following the marked lines on the back of the mount.

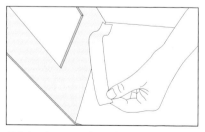

7 Join the top edge of the mount with the hardboard and apply a strip of masking tape along the join.

7 Align the top edge of the mount with the top edge of the hardboard. Apply a strip of double-sided masking tape along the length of the join. This will securely hinge the two pieces together.

8 On the reverse side of the picture, place two or three tabs of masking tape on the top edge so that half the tab is sticking to the picture.

9 Turn the picture over and position it on the hardboard. Attach a scrap of paper over the masking tape so that it does not stick to the mount and the paper can be removed later on. Bring over the mount and align the picture in the window. Ensure the picture is straight and there is an even overlap on each side. Place a small weight through the window onto the picture, taking care not to mark it.

10 Swing the mount back over the weight away from the picture and apply another tab of masking tape to each of the exposed tabs, forming a T-shaped hinge. The picture is now securely mounted.

MOUNT BORDERS

When using mounts you must decide the amount of border you want to be visible. Generally, borders are between 50 and 90 mm wide. Many framers make the bottom border measurement slightly larger than the other three sides which should be equal. This is to compensate for the visual illusion that the space at the bottom of the picture is smaller than the space at the top. If the same measurement is used all round this can have the effect of making the picture appear to have 'dropped' slightly in the frame. Some framers suggest an increase of 20 per cent at the bottom, although again this can vary. For example, if your border measurement for the top and sides is 70 mm, then the bottom measurement could be 85 mm. Make sure that the increase is noticeably larger, otherwise it may look as though you have made a mistake.

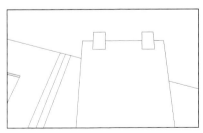

8 Position the tabs of masking tape on the top edge so that half the tab is sticking to the picture.

10 Apply another tab of masking tape to each of the exposed tabs to form a T-shaped hinge.

A mitre saw is used to cut 45 degree angles in the moulding. The pieces are then glued and nailed together. This frame has been constructed using a plain moulding and finished with a wood stain.

Cutting and joining moulding

The lengths of timber moulding can now be cut and joined to make the frame. A mitre saw is used to cut the moulding into lengths which are then glued together and held in place with a framing clamp until the adhesive has dried.

CALCULATING THE AMOUNT OF MOULDING

1 There is a simple formula for calculating how much moulding you need to make a frame. Calculate twice the width of the picture, plus twice the depth (or height), plus eight times the width of the mitre of the moulding (i.e. the distance from the rebate area to the back) to allow for wastage.

If you are making a frame for a picture measuring 300 x 200 mm, and the moulding has a 20 mm wide rebate, your calculations are as follows:

300 mm x 2 = 600 mm
200 mm x 2 = 400 mm
20 mm x 8 = 160 mm

The total is 1160 mm.

EQUIPMENT
● Moulding
● Tape measure or ruler
● Mitre saw
● Pencil
● Eraser
● Framing clamp
● PVA wood adhesive
● Small piece of rag
● Drill and 1 mm bit
● Panel pins
● Pin hammer
● Nail punch

If you add 10 per cent in length for safety, the total amount needed is 1276 mm or 1.276 m of moulding.

CHOOSING MOULDING

When choosing moulding for your frame, bear in mind the style of the picture and perhaps the style of decor in the room in which it will hang. For example, if the picture is to hang in the dining room, you may want to choose a moulding in a timber that matches the table. Also consider the size of the picture as this will determine the width of the moulding. Generally the bigger the picture is, the wider the moulding should be.

There will usually be one or two picture framing suppliers in your area that stock a variety of mouldings. Alternatively, some hardware or DIY stores now stock a range of mouldings that are suitable for framing.

CUTTING THE MOULDING

2 Slide the moulding into the mitre saw from the left-hand side, with the top of the moulding facing up and the rebate facing you. Hold the moulding firmly in position (some mitre saws have a device to help with this) and, with the blade on the left-hand side, cut the first mitre. No measurements need to be taken at this stage.

3 Swing the blade to the other side of the mitre saw so that the next cut is in the opposite direction. With the moulding on a flat surface, measure from the edge of the rebate of the first cut and mark the required length. Add 2 mm to your width and depth measurements to allow the backing and mount to fit comfortably in the frame, otherwise the frame will be too tight.

> CUTTING THE MOULDING
>
> When cutting moulding, start by cutting the longest length first, then if you do make a mistake, you can reuse the piece for the shorter length.

4 Slide the length of moulding along the mitre saw until the pencil mark is aligned with the blade. Cut the second mitre.

5 You now have to make a new 45 degree angle on the remaining length of moulding. Slide the moulding slightly further along and swing the blade to the other side of the mitre saw. Again, you don't need to take any measurements: you are simply removing an angle that cannot be used.

6 Place the length of moulding onto a flat surface and place the first piece of moulding alongside so that the rebate areas are adjacent. Align the two ends and then mark the remaining length. Remembering to change the saw blade to the other side of the mitre saw, place the length of moulding in the saw and cut as before.

7 Repeat the previous steps to cut the two short lengths. The four lengths of moulding are now ready to be glued together.

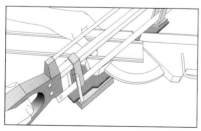

2 Hold the moulding in position and, with the blade on the left-hand side, cut the first mitre.

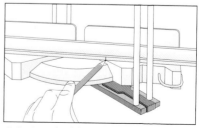

3 Swing the blade to the other side of the saw and measure from the edge of the rebate of the first cut.

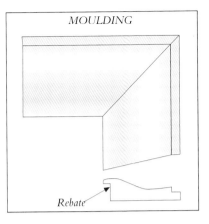

JOINING THE MOULDING

8 Place the four sides of the moulding together and place the framing clamp around them. Before applying the adhesive, tighten the framing strap and make sure that the corners fit neatly together. At this stage you can transpose the long or short pieces in order to achieve continuity as the intensity of stain or type of finish may vary slightly over the length.

9 Slacken off the clamp and apply adhesive to all four corners. Re-tighten the strap. Wipe off any excess adhesive from the corners and leave for about 20 minutes to set.

10 Remove the clamp and wipe off any remaining adhesive with a rag. Leave the frame overnight to allow the adhesive to reach full strength. If there are any slight gaps, these can be filled with a coloured wood filler. Alternatively, apply a little extra adhesive to the gap, wait a few minutes, and carefully wipe off the excess. The adhesive dries to a 'cloudy' appearance and will look better than a gap.

11 The adhesive is the main component that holds the frame together. However, it is advisable to also nail the corners for added strength. This can be done after the adhesive has dried. Stand the frame on its end and, about 10 mm from the corner, drill a 1 mm hole half the length of the panel pin you are using.

12 Hammer in the panel pin with the pin hammer and recess it slightly using a nail punch. The hole may then be filled using a wood filler.

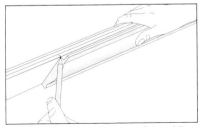

6 Place the second piece of moulding alongside the first. Align the two ends and mark the remaining length.

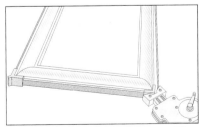

8 Place the four sides of the moulding together and fix the framing clamp around them.

A sheet of glass in front of the picture prevents dust entering the frame and, to some degree, helps to protect the picture from fading.

Cutting glass

Cutting glass is not difficult and requires only a few, inexpensive tools. The best glass cutters are fluid-filled and use a very light oil such as sewing machine oil. The cutting wheel is automatically lubricated every time it is used and, with care, will last for many years. There are cheaper versions also available.

EQUIPMENT

- Sheet of glass
- Felt-tipped pen (fine point)
- Metal straight-edge or ruler, and pencil
- Glass cutter
- Sharpening stone

METHOD

1 Lay the glass on a padded surface. Mark the dimensions on the glass with a pen and ruler. The glass should be the same size as the mount.

2 Using a ruler and the glass cutter, score along the marked line. Press firmly on the cutter, sufficient to make a clear 'splintering' sound as the cutter scores into the glass.

3 Place the glass over a pencil or the raised edge on the straight edge rule, aligning it with the scored line. With your hand pressing on one side, give the other side a firm tap. The glass should break cleanly and easily. Repeat for the second measurement.

4 To make the glass safer for handling, lightly run a sharpening stone several times over the edges.

HINT

Practise a few cuts on some spare glass before cutting the piece for your picture. Alternatively, have your local glass merchant cut the glass to size for you. This is relatively inexpensive.

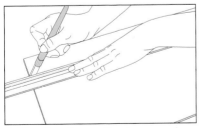

2 Use the glass cutter to score along the marked line. Press firmly on the cutter to make a 'splintering' sound.

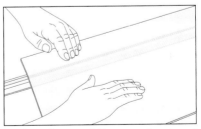

3 Place the scored line over the edge of the straight-edge (or pencil) and tap your hand on the glass to break it.

Assembling the frame

Now the individual components of the picture—the glass, mount, picture and backing board—are ready to be inserted into the frame. Check that the mount board is free of any pencil marks or fingerprints and use an eraser to gently rub them out.

EQUIPMENT

- Glass (cut to size)
- Glass cleaner
- Lint-free cloth
- Picture mount and backing board
- Frame
- Pin hammer or brad driver
- Panel pins
- Self-adhesive brown backing tape (48 mm wide)
- Pencil
- Drill and 1 mm drill bit or bradawl
- Two D-rings
- Two 6 mm or 8 mm screws
- Screwdriver
- Hanging wire

METHOD

1 Clean the glass with cleaner and a lint-free cloth. Lay the picture assembly on a flat surface and place the glass on top. Place the frame on top and turn the whole picture over so that it is now lying face down.

2 Using the pin hammer or brad driver, tap in a panel pin in the middle of each side. Turn the picture over for a final check. If you are satisfied, fix the remaining panel pins along the inside of the frame spacing the pins at 60–70 mm intervals.

3 Seal around the edge at the back of the frame with brown backing tape. This not only neatens the back but prevents dust and insects getting into the back of the frame. Self-adhesive tape is the best for this purpose as the gummed paper type may peel off after a few months.

4 The D-rings are positioned about one-third of the way down from the top of the frame. Mark their positions and make starter holes with a drill or bradawl. This makes it easier to screw in the two D-rings. Thread the hanging wire through each D-ring. The picture is now ready to hang.

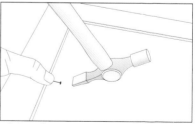

2 Working on the back of the frame, use the pin hammer to tap a pin in the middle of each side.

This picture shows an excellent combination of a light-coloured mount with a darker frame. The cream mount tones in well with the background of the picture while the dark frame complements the central design.

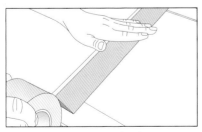

3 Seal the frame with backing tape to hide the pins and to prevent dust and insects getting into the frame.

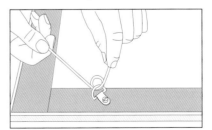

4 Screw in two D-rings on the sides of the frame and thread the hanging wire through the D-rings.

This somewhat formal arrangement of pictures has been softened by the use of ribbons tied into bows and glued onto the back of the frame. The ribbons do not support the pictures—they are merely decorative.

Hanging pictures

When it comes to hanging pictures in your home, consider not only whether the pictures should be grouped or given pride of place on a feature wall, but also the way in which they should be hung—with a hidden wire alone, or with a cord and decorative tassels, a chain or even with rope.

HOW TO HANG YOUR PICTURE

When hanging pictures there are a few basic points you should consider:

• Pick a suitable subject that reflects the style or ambience of the room. For example, a shell print is often suited to the bathroom; a beach scene works well in a conservatory.

• Consider the room's particular features. For instance, small pictures on a large wall could be lost unless they are grouped together.

• Pick a location that will display the picture to its best. If a picture is placed on a wall facing the door it becomes the first thing someone sees when entering the room.

• Experiment with arrangements of pictures. To do this, arrange groups of pictures on the floor in front of the wall on which they will hang. If you do this, it is easier to see how they will look when they are actually hung.

• Experiment with ways to hang your picture. Try hanging them on rope, chain, ribbons or even cord embellished with tassels.

• Consider the practicalities of hanging your pictures. An oil painting should never be placed above a heater as the rising heat may damage the surface of the painting. Similarly, exposure to long periods of sunlight may fade many pictures, particularly watercolours.

HANGING LARGE PICTURES

When hanging a large picture, hang it from two hooks, placing them about 30–40 cm apart, depending on the size of the picture. Hung this way the picture will never be crooked.

HINT

Try to avoid hanging pictures on exterior walls as these are prone to sharp changes in temperature. Over time, this could have a damaging effect on valuable artwork. Where this is not possible, create a gap between the back of the picture and the wall to increase airflow around the picture. Cut the cork from a wine bottle in half and fix the halves to the bottom corners. To compensate for this, ensure the picture hook or nail protrudes slightly further than normal so that the picture is straight.

Stained and waxed frame

If you buy plain timber moulding from a framing supplier, you will need to apply a finish to it. Wood stains will provide colour to the wood and a further application of a varnish or wax will protect the finish. The stain and wax are best applied to the moulding before it is joined, either to the complete length or the four cut pieces.

EQUIPMENT

- Small brush or soft cloth
- Wood stain
- Abrasive paper: fine grit
- Tack cloth and soft, lint-free cloth
- Furniture wax

METHOD

1 Using the small brush or soft cloth, apply the stain to the moulding. The stain will sink into the grain immediately. For a deeper colour apply a second coat of stain. Results will vary, depending on the stain and the type of wood used, so practise on a scrap piece of wood first to gain familiarity with the consistency and colour of the stain. Try to achieve a uniform look over the whole length of the moulding.

2 The stain may have the effect of raising the grain, making it feel slightly rough. If this is the case, use the abrasive paper to lightly sand the wood. Wipe away the dust.

3 When the stain is dry, use a lint-free cloth to sparingly apply the furniture wax. Buff the wax with the cloth until it reaches a soft sheen.

4 Join the moulding, following the instructions for cutting and joining moulding on page 11.

HINT

Your local hardware or DIY store will have a range of water- and oil-based wood stains to choose from. Oil-based wood stain is also available in undiluted form and can be diluted with methylated spirits to achieve the particular intensity of colour you want.

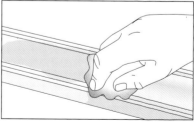

3 Apply the wax with a lint-free cloth and buff until the wax reaches a soft sheen.

A maple wood stain gives this timber frame a soft colour while a coat of wax protects the timber.

Two tones of green paint were used to paint this frame but contrasting colours could be used to complement a more abstract picture.

Painted frame

A coat of paint is one of the easiest methods of transforming a timber frame. To add interest to the frame choose two tones of the one colour and paint the frame alternating the two colours.

METHOD

1 Apply two coats of primer/undercoat to the length of moulding. Allow the paint to dry and then give the moulding a light sand. Do this *before* the moulding is cut into pieces.

2 Cut the moulding (see Cutting and joining moulding, page 11) and paint the four pieces of wood before they are assembled. Make sure that the paint does not cover the mitred ends or they will not join neatly. Paint two of the lengths light green and two dark green. Acrylic gloss-finish paint was used to paint our frame: you can also try ordinary acrylic paints or finish the frame with a gloss varnish.

3 Allow the paint to dry and join the moulding (see Joining the moulding, page 13).

EQUIPMENT

- Brush for primer/undercoat
- Acrylic primer/undercoat
- Moulding for frame
- Abrasive paper: fine grade
- 25 mm brush for top coat
- Acrylic gloss-finish paint: light green, dark green
- Water-based gloss varnish (optional)

HINT

When mixing paint colours to achieve different tones or colours, it is best to mix the darker shade of paint into the lighter shade. This way, you can gradually build up to achieve the correct shade without mixing more paint than is required for the project.

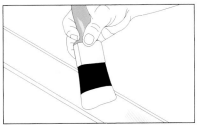

1 Apply two coats of primer/undercoat to the whole length of the moulding and allow the paint to dry.

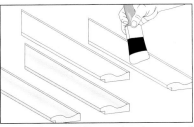

2 Cut the moulding and paint two of the lengths dark green and two lengths a lighter green.

Gilded frame

This striking gilded frame does not use genuine gold leaf but Dutch metal, a cheaper alternative that still gives impressive results. The paper-thin leaf is applied to a frame that has been coated with gilding size.

EQUIPMENT

- Frame
- Abrasive paper: fine grade
- Tack cloth
- Small brush for base coat
- Artists' acrylic paints: red oxide
- Water-based gilding size (see Gilding materials, page 26)
- Soft, white cotton gloves
- Dutch metal gold leaf
- Soft cloth or old silk scarf
- 25 mm soft brush for varnish
- Water-based satin varnish

METHOD

1 Sand the frame with the fine abrasive paper to ensure the surface is very smooth. Any small bumps or imperfections on the surface will be clearly visible under the fine gold leaf. Remove all the dust with the tack cloth.

2 Base coat the frame with two coats of red oxide, sanding lightly between coats. Remove any dust with the tack cloth and allow the frame to dry. A red base coat enhances the depth of the gold leaf.

3 Apply a smooth, even coat of gilding size to the frame (see box on Gilding materials, page 26). The size usually takes 15–20 minutes to dry but drying time will depend on the weather. Size does not dry completely but becomes slightly tacky, enough to grip the leaf. When testing the size to see if it is ready, use your knuckle

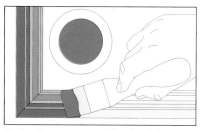

2 Apply two coats of red oxide paint to the frame, sanding between coats, and allow it to dry.

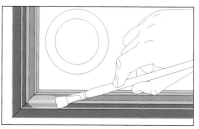

3 Apply a smooth coat of gilding size and allow it to dry. This usually takes 15–20 minutes.

The application of gold leaf to a frame can transform it into quite a showpiece, but make sure the style of artwork you are planning to put in it complements such an opulent style of frame.

GILDING MATERIALS

GILDING LEAF

Leaf for gilding can be purchased in booklets interleaved with tissue paper or in books where each sheet is mounted on backing paper. Genuine gold leaf is more expensive than imitation gold leaf or Dutch metal. Silver leaf is a suitable alternative to gold leaf.

GILDING SIZE

The gilding size acts as an adhesive for the gold leaf and is available as a water- or oil-based medium. A water-based sizing medium is easier to clean up than an oil-based medium, dries quickly and retains its tackiness for a longer period of time.

BOLE

In traditional gilding, the red base coat used beneath the surface of the gold leaf was called 'bole', a red clay used to give warmth and depth to the gold leaf. Today, a more readily available material—a red, or reddish brown acrylic paint—produces a similar effect. For a completely different effect experiment with other colours such as dark green or dark blue under the leaf. Although they are not traditional, these colours can look wonderful showing through any small cracks or imperfections in the leaf.

to lightly tap the surface—the size should feel tacky, not wet. Do not use your finger as an impression of your fingerprint will be left in the size and may be visible under the thin leaf.

4 Wearing white cotton gloves, carefully apply the Dutch metal to the frame, one sheet at a time. Position the leaf over the frame and gently lower it onto the surface. It is a good idea to shut any windows as any slight breeze will blow the sheets around. (You may find the leaf easier to handle if you cut the sheet into smaller squares.) As soon as the leaf touches the sized surface it will bond and cannot be removed, so take your time with this step.

5 Use the soft cloth to press the leaf firmly onto the surface and to smooth out any wrinkles in the leaf.

6 Continue to apply the leaf, overlapping the sheets slightly to achieve a full coverage. When the frame is fully covered allow it to dry for 24 hours.

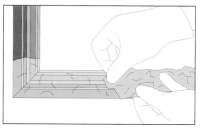

4 Wearing white cotton gloves, carefully apply the sheet of Dutch metal to the frame.

7 When the frame is dry, use the soft cloth to wipe over the surface to remove any loose gold leaf. Any gaps can be filled in with skewings (small left-over pieces of gold leaf). Alternatively, allowing small areas of the red base coat to show through can enhance the look of the frame.

8 The fragile Dutch metal needs to be protected or it will tarnish or rub off. Use the soft brush to apply two coats of varnish to the frame. Water-based varnish will keep the clarity of the gold leaf, whereas oil-based varnish will mellow your work, giving it an aged appearance.

The warm, earthy tones of the red base coat showing through the cracks of the Dutch metal enhance the richness of the gold.

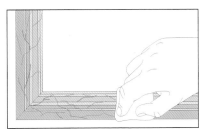

7 When the frame is dry, use the cloth to wipe over the surface to remove any loose pieces of leaf.

HANDLING GOLD LEAF

Gold leaf is extremely fragile and can easily be tarnished or torn. When handling gold leaf always wear cotton gloves as the oils in the skin may discolour the leaf. Alternatively, dust talcum powder over your hands. The talc will help to absorb the oil.

Craquelure frame

When two types of varnish are applied over the top of each other, the different drying times cause small cracks to form. By rubbing brown oil paint into the cracks, or crazes, the aged appearance is emphasised.

EQUIPMENT

- Frame
- Abrasive paper: fine grade
- Tack cloth
- Artists' acrylic paints: metallic gold, white pearl
- Small brush for base coat
- Two-part crackle varnish: antique varnish (part 1), crackle varnish (part 2)
- Soft, lint-free cloth
- Oil paint: burnt umber
- Brush for varnish
- Oil-based varnish

METHOD

1 Sand the frame to ensure the surface is smooth. Remove all the dust with a tack cloth.

2 Apply two even coats of metallic gold paint and allow it to dry. Apply one coat of white pearl and allow it to dry. (For a 'distressed' effect, lightly sand the frame with abrasive paper to reveal areas of the gold base coat.)

3 Using the base coat brush apply one coat of the antique varnish (part 1) and allow it to become dry to touch.

4 Before the antique varnish is completely dry, apply a coat of the crackle varnish (part 2) and allow it to dry. This can take up to 24 hours. The cracks will not appear until the varnish is almost dry.

5 To antique the frame, use the lint-free cloth to rub burnt umber oil paint over the entire surface of the frame. Rub lightly over the surface to remove the excess paint, leaving a light film of paint in the cracks and over areas of the frame. If desired, build up the intensity of antiquing by repeating this step. Allow the paint to dry thoroughly.

6 Using the varnish brush, apply a coat of oil-based varnish to protect the work.

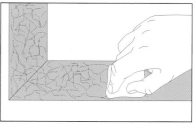

5 Use the cloth to rub burnt umber oil paint over the frame to emphasise the small cracks.

A craquelure finish is applied to this frame to produce the illusion that it is an antique. The fine fractures on the surface of the frame are emphasised by rubbing a little burnt umber oil paint into them.

Gluing wooden shapes onto a frame is an inexpensive way of decorating an otherwise plain frame. Wooden shapes are available from craft stores and are available in a variety of designs.

Decorated frame

Give a quick 'pick-me-up' to a plain wooden frame by gluing wooden shapes around it and spraying it with gold paint. If the frame is for a child's room you may want to use wooden numbers and paint the frame using primary colours.

METHOD

1 Use the fine abrasive paper to sand the frame and the wooden tulips and hearts so the edges are smooth and even. Wipe away the dust with the tack cloth.

2 Use the tape measure and pencil to mark even spaces around the frame for positioning the wooden pieces.

3 Apply adhesive to the underside of the tulips and hearts and press them onto the marked positions. Alternate the positions of the tulips and the hearts. Allow the adhesive to dry.

4 Give the frame one coat of cream paint, remembering to paint the inside and outside edges of the frame. Allow the paint to dry.

5 Hold the can of gold spray paint 20–25 cm from the surface of the frame and spray a light, even coat of paint over the frame. Continue to spray until the frame is fully covered. Allow the paint to dry thoroughly.

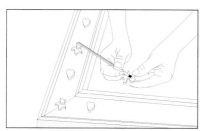

3 Apply PVA adhesive onto the backs of the wooden shapes and press them onto the frame.

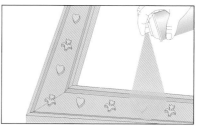

5 Holding the can a short distance away from the surface, spray the frame with the gold spray paint.

Distressed frame

The art of 'distressing' can add immediate romance to an otherwise plain item. For truly 'authentic' distressing, use a nail to add a few dints and scratches to the surface before painting it.

METHOD

1 Sand the frame to smooth the surface. Use the tack cloth to wipe all the excess dust off the frame.

2 Base coat the frame with two coats of aqua paint, sanding the frame lightly after the first coat has dried.

3 Apply two coats of cobalt blue, sanding lightly after the first coat.

4 Wrap the wet-and-dry abrasive paper around the cork block and briefly immerse the block in water. Working in the one direction, gently sand the surface to gradually remove the top coats of paint and reveal areas of the aqua base coat. In some areas, particularly the 'high' areas of the frame, you may want to sand through to expose areas of the wood.

EQUIPMENT

- Frame
- Abrasive paper: fine grade, fine grade wet-and-dry
- Tack cloth
- Brush for base coat
- Artists' acrylic paints: aqua, cobalt blue
- Cork sanding block
- Thin kitchen cloth
- Soft brush for varnish
- Water-based matt varnish

5 Use a damp kitchen cloth to wash away any paint residue before varnishing the frame.

6 To finish the frame, apply two to three coats of water-based varnish. Allow the varnish to dry thoroughly between each coat.

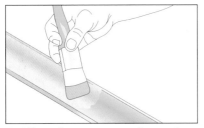

3 Allow the two coats of aqua base coat to dry and then apply two coats of cobalt blue.

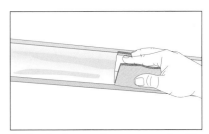

4 Sand the surface to gradually remove the top coats of paint and reveal areas of the aqua base coat.

A combination of blue and aqua paint works well on this distressed frame but you may like to try other combinations such as yellow over a cream base coat or navy over a red base coat.

The pale green sponging on this frame is enhanced by the addition of a raised stencilled design. Brown oil paint is lightly rubbed over the raised areas to give the frame an antiqued appearance.

Low-relief frame

To create this interesting three-dimensional design, texture paste is applied through a stencil. When dry, the low-relief design is antiqued using oil paint.

EQUIPMENT

- Frame
- Abrasive paper: fine grade
- Tack cloth and soft cloth
- Brush for base coat
- Artists' acrylic paints: white pearl, jade
- Palette
- Sponge
- Paper towel
- Purchased stencil (see box, page 37)
- Low-tack tape
- Palette knife
- Texture paste
- Burnt Umber oil paint
- Oil-based antiquing medium
- Gold wax paste
- Soft brush for varnish
- Oil-based varnish

ALTERNATIVE

To achieve a faux carved wood finish, try this technique. Base coat the frame with yellow and apply the texture paste through the stencil. When the paste is dry, brush over the frame with watery brown acrylic paint. Wipe off the excess paint with a rag.

SPONGING THE FRAME

1 Use the abrasive paper to sand the frame to ensure the surface is smooth. Remove all the dust from the frame with the tack cloth.

2 Base coat the frame with white pearl paint and allow it to dry.

3 Place equal portions of jade and white pearl paint on the palette. Moisten the sponge and dab it into both colours. Blot the sponge onto a paper towel to remove the excess paint before applying the paint to the frame. Sponge the colour onto the frame, moving your hand slightly from side to side so that both colours are blended. Continue to sponge the paint onto the frame until the desired intensity of colour is reached. Allow the paint to dry.

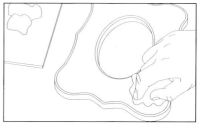

3 Dip the sponge into the jade and white pearl paint, dab off the excess and apply it to the frame.

When antiquing the frame allow the burnt umber paint to build up around the edges of the raised design.

APPLYING THE TEXTURE PASTE

4 Place the stencil in the desired position and hold it in place with low-tack adhesive tape, which will not damage the paint when it is removed. Use the palette knife to spread the texture paste over the stencil. The technique used is similar to icing a cake. The paste will fill the cut-out sections of the stencil.

5 Smooth the surface of the paste with the palette knife and carefully lift the stencil off the frame. If desired, repeat this process to apply the design to the other sides of the frame. Allow the paste to dry for 24 hours. Clean the stencil and palette knife.

FINISHING

6 Apply a small amount of burnt umber oil paint to the frame. Use a cloth moistened with antiquing medium to spread the oil paint over the surface. Continue to wipe over the frame, gradually removing the oil paint until the desired amount of antiquing is reached.

7 As a finishing touch, squeeze a small amount of gold wax paste onto your finger and rub it around the edge of the frame. Allow the frame to dry for 24 hours to allow the antiquing medium to dry and cure.

8 Apply a coat of oil-based varnish to protect the finish.

CUTTING A STENCIL

Stencilling is one of the easiest ways to decorate a surface. There are many pre-cut stencils available from art or craft stores, all of which are perfectly suited to this frame, but it is very easy to cut your own stencil from a sheet of stencil plastic.

If you are unable to purchase a sheet of acetate, heavy card is a good alternative. Trace the design and transfer it onto the card using carbon paper. Cut out the design following steps 2–3.

1 Place the stencil plastic over your design and trace it using a felt-tipped pen. Tape the stencil plastic in position to prevent it from slipping.

2 Place the stencil plastic on a cutting mat. A self-healing cutting mat is best for this although a wad of newspapers can also make a good cutting mat.

3 Use a craft knife or scalpel to carefully cut around the drawn

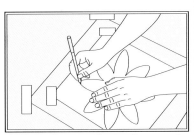

1 Tape the stencil plastic over the design and trace around it using a felt-tipped pen.

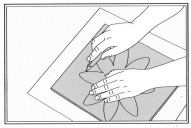

3 Place the stencil plastic on the cutting mat and carefully cut around the design with the craft knife.

design. Avoid lifting the knife away from the design as this is how the edges of the stencil become jagged. To achieve this smooth edge, keep the knife pressed into the mat as you cut.

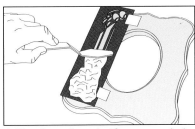

4 Use the palette knife to spread the paste over the stencil. The paste will fill the cut-out areas of the stencil.

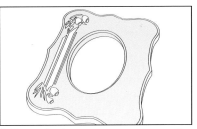

5 Smooth the texture paste so the surface is fairly flat and carefully peel off the stencil.

Cardboard frame

Not all frames are constructed from wood—cardboard is also an excellent medium for making a frame. This cardboard frame is decorated using a hot glue gun which is swirled randomly over the frame to create a lively, abstract design.

METHOD

1 Using the ruler and pencil, measure and mark a distance 6 cm in from each outside edge of the mount board to form a centre square.

2 Place the mount board on the cutting mat and use the craft knife and ruler to cut out the centre square. Set the square aside as this can be later used as the backing board.

3 Heat the hot glue gun and apply the glue to the mount board by swirling the glue over the surface to create a random pattern. If preferred, use a pencil to sketch in a rough outline of the design before applying the glue. If you are using dimensional paint instead of a hot glue gun, make a large hole in the tip of the tube so the paint flow is thicker.

4 Allow the glue to dry thoroughly and apply two coats of French blue paint to the frame.

5 Use the bristle brush to apply the gold wax paste over some of the raised areas to add highlights. If necessary, use a cloth to wipe off the excess paste.

EQUIPMENT

- Ruler
- Pencil
- 27 x 27 cm mount board or cardboard
- Cutting mat
- Craft knife
- Hot glue gun (or fabric dimensional paint)
- Artists' acrylic paint: French blue
- Cheap bristle brush
- Gold wax paste
- Lint-free cloth
- Brush for varnish
- Water-based satin varnish

6 Apply two coats of varnish to protect the surface, allowing the first coat to dry thoroughly before applying the second.

7 Insert the photo or artwork (if desired, add a mount and a piece of glass) and tape the backing board onto the back of the frame. For a standing frame, glue a rectangular piece of cardboard onto the back of the frame to support it. Alternatively, attach a picture hook to the back of the frame.

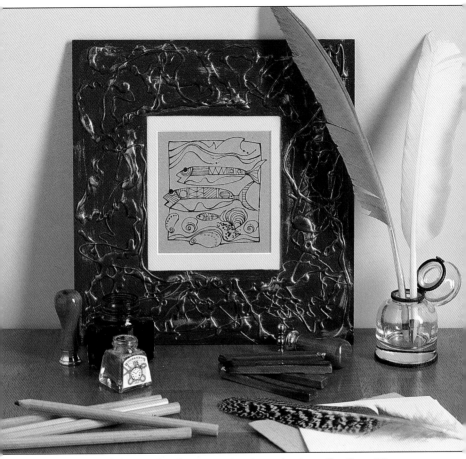

Hot glue is swirled over this frame to give it an 'embossed' effect. The same effect can also be achieved with fabric dimensional paint.

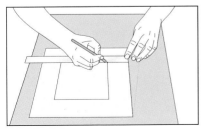

1 Measure and mark 6 cm in from the outside edge of the mount board to form a square.

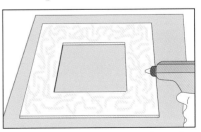

3 Heat the hot glue gun and swirl it over the frame to create a random, swirling design.

Textured cardboard frame

Cardboard is an inexpensive and versatile medium for frame-making. This fun three-dimensional frame is constructed from cardboard and is covered with a thick decorative paste. It was then finished with a coat of pink paint.

METHOD

1 Using the pencil and ruler, draw the pattern for the frame onto a piece of cardboard (see diagram on page 42).

2 Lay the cardboard on the cutting mat and, using the craft knife and ruler, cut out the centre square. Put the square aside; it can be used as the backing board once the picture is inserted into the frame.

3 Measure and divide each side into four equal sections. Use the craft knife to score along the marked lines—do not cut through the cardboard.

4 Fold the cardboard inwards along the scored edge to form the shape of the frame. Hold it in position with masking tape.

EQUIPMENT
● Pencil
● Ruler
● Cardboard
● Cutting mat
● Craft knife
● Masking tape
● PVA adhesive
● Newspaper
● Old brush for applying adhesive
● Palette knife
● Texture paste
● Acrylic paint: pink
● Palette
● Stencil brush
● Paper towel
● Brush for varnish
● Water-based varnish

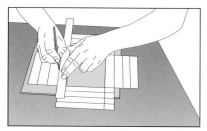

3 Divide each side into four sections. Use the craft knife to score along the marked lines.

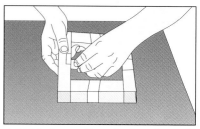

4 Fold the cardboard edges inwards along the scored lines to form the frame and tape to hold in position.

A bright, textured cardboard frame teamed with a pretty gerbera print make this frame an effective decoration for a teenager's bedroom—and it's very economical to make.

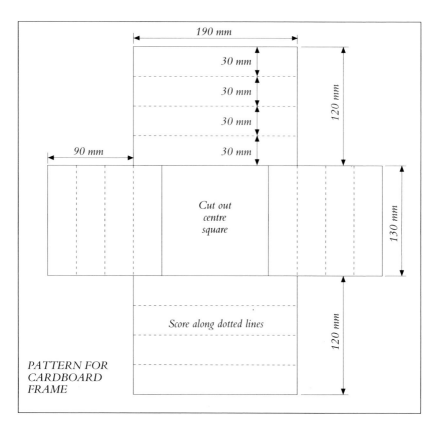

PATTERN FOR
CARDBOARD
FRAME

(Pattern labels: 190 mm, 30 mm, 30 mm, 30 mm, 30 mm, 120 mm, 90 mm, 130 mm, 120 mm, *Cut out centre square*, *Score along dotted lines*)

DECORATING FRAMES

There's no limit to what you can do to decorate a frame. Try these few simple ideas. All that is needed is some adhesive, some odds and ends for decorating and a few ideas to spark the imagination.

- Glue colourful beads, strings of pearls or cabochons around the frame. Arrange the beads in swirling patterns or in colourful geometric designs.

- Nature provides plenty of inspiration as well as being a great source of items for decorating frames. To decorate a frame that has a seaside theme, glue small shells or pieces of driftwood around the frame. Other ideas include gluing nuts, leaves or small pine cones on the frame.

- Buttons, varying in size, shape or colour, can be glued around a frame. Leave the frame as a bright medley of coloured buttons or allow the adhesive to dry thoroughly and spray paint the whole frame in a colour to suit your decor.

5 Mix PVA adhesive and water at a ratio of 4:1. Tear the newspaper into small pieces and soak them in the adhesive and water mixture. Remove the pieces from the mixture and stick them around the frame.

6 Use an old brush to apply two coats of the adhesive mix over the torn newspaper and allow it to dry.

7 Using a palette knife, generously apply the texture paste to the front, sides and back of the frame. The surface should be textured and uneven. Allow the paste to dry.

8 Place a small amount of pink paint on the palette. Dab the stencil brush into the paint and blot the brush on paper towel to remove the excess paint. Apply the paint to the frame, dabbing the brush over the uneven texture to achieve a full coverage.

9 Allow the paint to dry and apply several coats of satin varnish to protect the textured finish. Glue the picture onto the backing board and tape onto the frame.

Pink paint is applied over the textured surface of the frame using a stencil brush.

DECORATING ALTERNATIVE
There are many ways of decorating a cardboard frame such as this. Follow the instructions to make the basic frame (steps 1–6) and allow it to dry. Use modelling clay to make shapes (stars, circles or hearts are simple but effective) or cut shapes from cardboard. Glue the shapes around the frame. Base coat the frame in white and paint as desired. Varnish with two to three coats of satin varnish.

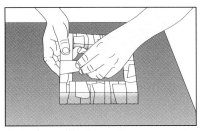

5 Soak small pieces of newspaper in the adhesive and water mixture and stick them around the frame.

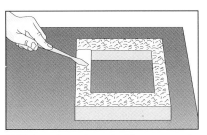

7 Using the palette knife, generously apply the texture paste to the front, sides and back of the frame.

Colourful painted flowers on a deep blue background make this frame a lively addition to any interior.

Papier-mâché frame

Papier-mâché, literally meaning 'chewed paper', is a technique of constructing three-dimensional objects using adhesive and pieces of paper. The paper can also be shredded in a blender and mixed with adhesive to form a pulp which is pressed into a mould.

MAKING THE PULP

It is easy to make your own papier-mâché pulp and it is an excellent way of recycling old newspapers or shredded office paper into useful and decorative items for the home. A blender, strainer, adhesive and water are all that is needed to make the pulp but, if preferred, ready-made pulp can be purchased from craft and art stores.

1 Separate the shredded paper slightly (so water will reach all of it), and check that there aren't shredded bits of plastic (e.g. from envelope windows) in the paper. Place the paper in the bucket and cover with boiling water. Leave overnight.

2 For a finer textured pulp, strain off the cooled water and repeat step 1. Alternatively, boil the pulp in a saucepan for about 15 minutes with sufficient water to cover it.

3 Place small amounts of the paper pulp in the blender and liquidise it until the paper is broken down. You will probably need to add more water, a little at a time, to facilitate the blending process.

4 Strain the pulp through a strainer or with your fingers so that the excess water is removed.

5 Place the pulp in a mixing bowl and gradually add the adhesive. (If using wallpaper adhesive, use approximately ½ to ¾ of a litre—see

4 Strain the pulp through a strainer or with your fingers so that the excess water is removed.

Adhesives, page 48.) You can add whiting (2 tablespoons per half litre of adhesive) for added strength.

6 Use your fingers to mix the pulp and adhesive together until the mixture reaches a soft, clay-like consistency. This step must be done by hand as mechanical mixers will not give the same result. The pulp should not be too wet or it will be difficult to handle and will not dry to its proper strength. Use the pulp immediately but it can be stored overnight—cover with cling film or place it in an air-tight container.

FRAME MOULDS

A variety of household and kitchen items can be used as moulds to make papier-mâché frames. Although plastic is perhaps the easiest to manage as it has an amount of 'give' and will release the pulp easily, stainless steel, glass and even wooden moulds can be used. Plastic food containers, trays and serving platters are also good options. Some of these have raised patterns which can add interest to the finished frame.

When choosing a mould keep in mind that you will be applying the pulp to the inside so ensure there are no 'undercuts' which will make it difficult to remove. If using moulds that are not plastic or glass, be sure to coat them with an ample amount of petroleum jelly so the papier-mâché can be easily removed.

This project uses a plastic pot plant saucer as the frame mould.

TROUBLESHOOTING

WET PULP

If the finished pulp is sloppy and difficult to manage you may have too much water in the mixture. Make sure to squeeze out as much water as you can before adding the adhesive and whiting. As a last resort, add more squeezed pulp to the mixture.

HARD PULP

If the finished pulp is too hard, either add more adhesive to the pulp mixture, or dip your hands in the adhesive and manipulate the pulp to achieve a smooth finish.

RELEASING THE PULP

If the papier-mâché will not release easily from the mould it may not be dry. Leave it for a while longer and if it still won't drop out, you may not have put enough petroleum jelly in the mould. Try flexing the mould slightly or tapping it with a rubber hammer over the area where it seems to be stuck.

As a last resort, try spinning the papier-mâché around as you hold the mould. If a small area of the papier-mâché becomes stuck it can be patched with wood filler.

If using moulds that are not plastic or glass be sure to coat them with approximately double the amount of petroleum jelly that you would normally use.

EQUIPMENT FOR FRAME

- Frame moulds: pot plant saucer of desired size, smaller pot plant saucer (at least 8 cm smaller)
- Petroleum jelly
- House brick or weight
- Papier-mâché pulp (see Making the pulp, page 45)
- Round chocolate moulds
- PVA adhesive
- Spoon or flat knife for shaping
- Abrasive paper: fine grade
- Water-based sealer or acrylic primer/undercoat
- Wood filler for fine gaps (optional)
- Brushes: 25 mm brush for base coat, no. 5 flat, liner
- Acrylic paints: green, white, red, blue, yellow, black
- Pencil
- Carbon paper
- Tracing paper
- Stylus
- Cardboard
- Scissors
- 25 mm brush for varnish
- Water- or oil-based varnish

MAKING THE PAPIER-MÂCHÉ FRAME

1 Coat the inside of the large saucer and the outside rim of the smaller saucer with a thin film of petroleum jelly. This allows the pulp to release when it is dry.

2 Place the smaller saucer in the centre of the larger one. Place it upside down and weight it with a brick, or similar, so that it doesn't easily move.

3 Take small handfuls of the prepared pulp and press it into the gap between the two saucers. (The pulp can be purchased from art stores or it can be made following the instructions on page 45.) Press the pulp firmly into the sides of the saucer, being careful not to move the inside saucer or the inner edge of the frame will be uneven.

4 Work around the mould filling it with the papier-mâché pulp. Shape the pulp with your fingers or the back of a spoon to achieve the desired shape.

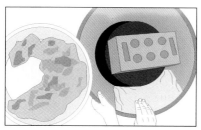

3 Take small handfuls of the prepared papier-mâché pulp and press it into the mould.

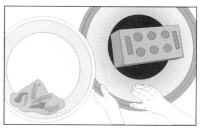

4 Fill the saucer with the pulp then shape it with your fingers to give the frame a bevelled edge.

THE HISTORY OF PAPIER-MÂCHÉ

The technique of recycling paper into papier-mâché is believed to have been invented in China in the second century AD. Items such as warrior's helmets, trunks and screens were all moulded from papier-mâché. By the eighteenth century the technique of making papier-mâché items had spread to Europe, Russia, North Africa and the USA. Today, papier-mâché crafts are enjoying a revival—it is a very inexpensive and versatile medium.

5 When complete, carefully remove the inner saucer and smooth the edge. The saucer must be removed before the pulp dries completely or it will shrink around it and be difficult to remove.

6 Coat the round chocolate moulds with petroleum jelly and fill them with pulp to make the small half circles for the flower centres. (The outside diameter of this frame is 38 cm and eight circles were needed.)

ADHESIVE

Wallpaper adhesive is available in powdered form and is mixed with water. It can be purchased from hardware, DIY paint and art stores.

Heavy-duty wallpaper paste should not be used when making papier-mâché pulp as it contains a fungicide.

7 Place the papier-mâché in the sun or a warm place to dry. It may take up to a week to dry completely.

8 When the surface of the papier-mâché is dry (after a day or two) but still soft underneath, burnish it with the back of a spoon dipped in adhesive. This will compact the pulp, making a smoother and stronger finished piece. The papier-mâché must be completely dry before it is painted or moisture will seep to the surface and the paint will flake off. Check it does not 'give' when you push on it before you continue.

9 When it is completely dry, glue the round half circles around the frame, spacing them approximately 10 cm apart, though this will depend on the size of the frame.

PAINTING THE FRAME

10 Lightly sand the edges of the frame and use a cloth to brush off the dust thoroughly. Seal the frame with a water-based sealer or acrylic primer/undercoat. If desired, fill any imperfections with a wood filler.

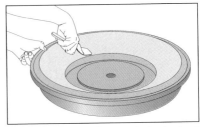

8 Burnish the surface with the back of a spoon dipped in adhesive. This will help to compact the pulp.

A black outline is painted around the petals and centres of the flowers to give them definition.

11 Base coat the frame using green paint and allow it to dry. Apply a second coat of paint if necessary to achieve an even coverage. Allow the paint to dry thoroughly before transferring the pattern onto it.

12 Use the carbon paper and pencil to trace the design for the flower from page 62 and transfer it onto cardboard using a stylus. Cut out the flower shape.

13 Using the cardboard as a template, place it on the frame and draw around the shape of the flower. Draw the flowers around the frame, overlapping the petals if necessary.

14 Paint the flowers, first using a coat of white paint, and then using two coats of each colour to achieve a solid coverage. Use a liner brush and black paint to outline the flowers, adding small dots to the centre of each flower. Allow the paint to dry.

15 Apply at least two protective coats of varnish in a gloss, satin or matt finish, according to taste.

16 Fix a mirror or an image to the back of the frame. Support the image by mounting it on cardboard or plywood before attaching it to the back of the frame. Mount the frame onto cardboard (if using an image) or onto plywood (if using a mirror) and glue it to the frame using a strong adhesive. If mounting a mirror also attach some screws to the back of the frame. For added strength, glue the screws into the frame.

9 Glue the papier-mâché half circles around the frame, spacing them approximately 10 cm apart.

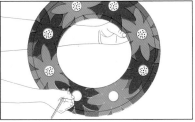

14 Use a liner brush and black paint to outline the flowers. Place small black dots in the flowers' centre.

While découpage does require patience in cutting out images and applying layers of varnish, the results are truly stunning. The religious theme of this paper complements the icon-like frame but many other papers are also suitable.

Découpaged frame with shutters

This frame with shutters was decorated using a combination of sponging and découpage techniques. It was made by attaching two shutters—a single piece of MDF board was cut in half—to a basic wooden frame. The découpage is added after the frame and shutters have been sponged.

EQUIPMENT FOR FRAME
• 1.5 m of moulding
• 12 mm thick medium density fibreboard (MDF)
• Ruler and pencil
• Jigsaw or handsaw
• G-cramps
• 4 x 25 mm brass hinges
• Drill
• Screwdriver

MAKING THE FRAME

1 Using the length of moulding, make a basic frame as described in Cutting and joining moulding, page 11. Choose a moulding with a flat profile for this project as it ensures the shutters close neatly. The dimensions of the frame used for this project are 250 x 250 mm but you may wish to make your frame smaller or larger than this.

2 Starting with a 12 mm thick sheet of MDF, measure and mark a square 250 x 250 mm. Use the frame as a template if you prefer.

3 Using the jigsaw or handsaw, cut along the marked lines. You now have a square of MDF the same size as the frame.

4 Rule a line down the middle of the board and cut it in half to make the two shutters. Position the two halves on top of the frame and clamp them securely with the G-cramps.

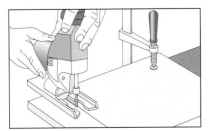

3 Mark a square 250 x 250 mm and use the jigsaw or handsaw to cut along the drawn lines.

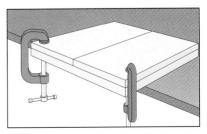

4 Cut the square in half and place the pieces on the frame. Use the G-cramps to hold them in place.

EQUIPMENT FOR DÉCOUPAGE

- Frame with shutters (see Making the frame, page 51)
- Brush for base coat
- Abrasive paper: fine grade
- Tack cloth
- Artists' acrylic paints: white pearl, storm blue, dioxazine purple
- Iridescent tinting medium
- Palette
- Sponge
- Paper towel
- Low-tack tape
- 25 mm brush for sealer
- Water-based sealer (see box on sealing papers, page 54)
- Good quality 4 inch curved cuticle scissors
- Découpage paper (see box on découpage papers, page 54)
- PVA adhesive
- Water
- Roller
- Good quality varnish
- Craft knife or scalpel

5 With the cramps still in place, mark and drill the holes for the hinges. Make sure all four hinges are attached before removing the cramps.

6 Your frame with shutters is now complete. A small brass clasp can be used as a finishing touch if required.

ADDING THE DÉCOUPAGE

7 Remove the hinges from the frame and set them aside. Base coat the frame and shutters with two coats of white pearl paint. Lightly sand the surface after the first coat has dried.

8 Place storm blue and dioxazine purple acrylic paint plus Iridescent tinting medium on a palette. Using the sponge, pick up the storm blue and a small amount of both the purple and Iridescent tinting medium. Blot the excess paint off onto a paper towel. Apply the paint to the frame and shutters making the paint darker on the outer edges and lighter towards the middle. The tinting medium gives a translucence to the paints so more is used towards the centre of the image to create a

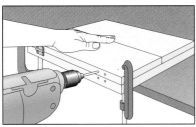

5 Mark and drill the holes for the hinges. Make sure all hinges are attached before removing the cramps.

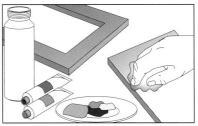

8 Use the sponge to apply the mix of blue, purple and tinting medium to all sides of the frame and shutters.

'radiance' around Mary. Allow the paint to dry thoroughly and use the fine grade abrasive paper to lightly sand the surface. Wipe away the dust.

9 Paint around the edges of the shutters and the frame with storm blue and dioxazine purple.

10 Mask off a thin stripe around the outer and inner edges of the frame with low-tack tape. Sponge a lighter stripe with tinting medium and a small amount of storm blue and dioxazine purple.

11 Seal both the front and back of all the découpage papers with sealer (see box on sealing papers, page 54) and allow them to dry thoroughly.

12 Using the découpage scissors, and holding the point away from you, carefully cut around the outline of the angels and Mary for the front of the shutters (or if using another image, remove the background). Cut around the images of the angels for inside the shutters. For best results, take time with cutting out.

Tinting medium adds translucence to the paints so more is added to create the 'light' radiating around Mary.

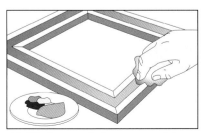

10 *Mask around the outer and inner edges of the frame and sponge a lighter stripe around the middle.*

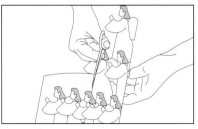

12 *Holding the point of the scissors away from you, carefully cut around the outline of the angels.*

DÉCOUPAGE HINTS

DÉCOUPAGE PAPERS

There are many beautiful découpage papers available and this project presents only one idea—images of fruit or flowers could work equally well. The project pictured uses two copies of the same image. For the front of the shutters the images of Mary and the angels are required. (The background of the design has been cut away.) The inside surface of the shutters requires only the images of the angels. Alternatively, images can be colour photocopied, enlarging or decreasing the image to suit the size of the project.

SEALING PAPERS

Sealers are used to prevent the image smudging. There are many special sealers for découpage available, but you can also use PVA adhesive diluted with water (proportions of one part PVA to two parts water).

CUTTING OUT

Curved cuticle scissors or scissors with a fine point are essential for good cutting results. When cutting out the image, hold the scissors still and move the image through the blades. Work from under the image so you can clearly see where you are cutting.

13 Working on the inside of both shutters, glue the angels to the outer edge of the shutters. The adhesive mix used for decoupaging is PVA thinned with a little water. Increase the amount of PVA if using images from thicker paper or card. Use the roller to remove any air bubbles that may be trapped beneath the surface of the paper.

14 Allow the adhesive to dry and apply a coat of water-based sealer to the images. When the sealer has dried, apply several coats of varnish over the entire piece. Sand lightly between each coat of varnish and carefully wipe over the surface with the tack cloth.

15 Place the doors face up and closed together on the work surface. Following step 13, glue the image of Mary and the angels over both doors in one piece. When completely dry, cut down the middle of the doors with a craft knife or scalpel.

16 Apply a coat of sealer to the images and allow to dry. Following step 14, apply several coats of varnish.

13 Use the roller to remove any air bubbles that may be trapped beneath the surface of the image.

The shutters open to reveal a mirror though, if preferred, the mirror can be replaced with a painting or photograph.

Fabric covered frame

Cover frames using fabrics that co-ordinate with other soft furnishi
in the room. This frame is first padded and then covered with a p
blue check fabric.

METHOD

1 Place the frame face down onto the wadding and draw around the outside and inside edge of the frame. Cut out the wadding and set it aside.

2 Place the frame onto the fabric and again draw around the outside and inside of the frame. Use a pencil to do this as pen marks may be visible through the fabric. Using a ruler, draw a line 1.5 cm inside the inside edge. This will allow the fabric to be folded over the inner edge of the frame. Add a 3 cm allowance around the outer edge of the frame.

3 Cut out the fabric along the marked lines. Iron the fabric and place it right side down on the table.

4 Glue the wadding onto the front of the frame, then apply a light coat of adhesive onto the wadding and press the frame, wadding side down, onto the fabric, aligning it with the drawn lines. If the adhesive is applied too thickly it may be visible through the fabric. Smooth out the fabric.

5 Cut the outer corners of the fabric at 90 degrees to allow them to be turned over to the back of the frame.

EQUIPMENT

- Frame
- Wadding
- Scissors
- Ruler and pencil
- Fabric
- PVA adhesive and small brush
- Braid

Leave small tabs of fabric on the corners—these can be glued around the sides of the frame to make the corners neater. Snip small mitres at 45 degrees on the inside corners.

6 Apply adhesive to the back of the frame and turn the fabric over to the back. Start by gluing the tabs around the corners of the frame. To finish, glue some braid around the inside edge of the frame.

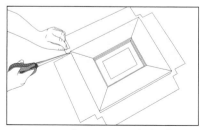

6 Cut out the corners of the fabric, leaving small tabs to be folded around the sides of the frame.

When covering a frame with fabric the trick is to use a thin frame so that after the fabric has been mitred and folded over the inner edge, only a minimal amount of bare frame will be visible in the corners.

The beauty of this punched metal frame lies in its simplicity—select one or two motifs and repeat them around the frame.

Punched metal frame

This punched metal frame takes its inspiration from a combination of the simple designs of the Shakers and the more elaborate designs favoured by the Mexicans and Indians. A thin sheet of aluminium is used to cover the frame and the design is punched with a nail and hammer. The key to success is to keep the design as simple as possible.

PREPARING THE FRAME

1 Base coat the front and sides of the frame using silver or grey acrylic paint. By using a paint similar in colour to the thin aluminium sheet, any areas where the aluminium does not completely cover the frame (such as the outer corners or the inside edge) will be better camouflaged. If you prefer you can paint the back of the frame as well.

COVERING THE FRAME

2 Place the sheet of aluminium on the towel. The towel prevents the soft aluminium sheet from being scratched. Position the frame face down on the aluminium.

3 Use the pen to trace around the outer and inner edges of the frame. The pen will leave an impression in the soft aluminium. Use the ruler and pen and draw an outer border measuring approximately 5 cm wide around the frame. This will allow the aluminium to be turned over to the back of the frame. Remove the frame and set it aside.

3 **Using the pen, draw a border approximately 5 cm wide around the outer edge of the frame.**

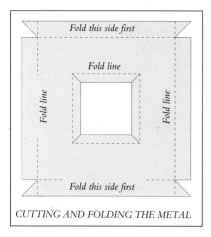

CUTTING AND FOLDING THE METAL

Cut angles in the four outer corners as shown in the diagram at left. Don't cut the corners at 90 degrees—the extra aluminium can be folded around the side of the frame and will make the corners neater.

6 Place the cut sheet of aluminium on the towel and position the frame on the aluminium, using the drawn lines for the inner edge of the frame as a positional guide.

4 Use a ruler and the pen to draw a border 1.2 cm wide around the inside. This is to allow for turning the aluminium around the rebate of the frame. The width of this inner border will vary according to the depth of the rebate so measure it first.

7 Turn the aluminium over the rebate on the inner edge of the frame and use tape to hold it in place. Fold one outer edge of the aluminium around the frame and onto the back. Use masking tape as a temporary measure to hold the sheet in position. If you make a mistake when you are punching the frame the aluminium can easily be removed and the frame re-covered. After the design has been completed the aluminium can be permanently secured with tacks. Fold the aluminium and tape the other three sides. Turn the frame to the front and check the aluminium is sitting evenly on the frame.

5 Wearing cotton gloves, use the scissors to cut out the marked inner frame. To begin, punch a hole in the centre with the point of the scissors and work the cut towards the marked line. Snip the inner corners of the aluminium sheet at a 45 degree angle.

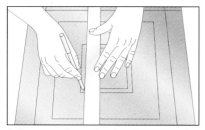

4 Draw an inner border 1.2 cm wide. The width will vary according to the depth of the rebate of the frame.

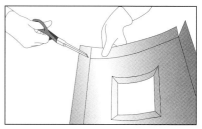

5 Cut the four corners of the aluminium so that it can be folded around to the back of the frame.

Use a small screwdriver to punch small, straight indents in the design.

a nail and hammer to punch holes in the aluminium. Try to space the holes evenly apart and maintain an even pressure when hammering the nail. The size of the nail and the amount of pressure used when hammering will affect the size of the holes so it is best to practise on a spare piece of aluminium before committing to the final piece. To add the 'petals' on the flowers around the sides of the frame, use a small screwdriver instead of a nail to make straight indentations.

8 Trace the design onto tracing paper, following the pattern on page 62. When tracing the design allow enough paper around the edge so that it can be wrapped around the frame. Position the design onto the front of the frame, fold the excess tracing paper around the frame and secure it with masking tape on the back.

PUNCHING THE ALUMINIUM

9 Place the frame face up on the towel and, following the design, use

10 Continue punching around the frame to complete the design. Check that all areas of the design have been completed before removing the tracing paper.

11 To finish the frame remove the masking tape from the back of the frame and hammer in small tacks along the edge of the aluminium. Work on one side at a time. Using smaller tacks, do the same around the inner edge of the frame. The size of tacks required will depend on the depth of the frame and the rebate.

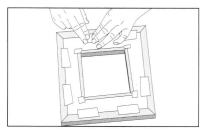

7 Turn the aluminium over the rebate and over the outer edge of the frame. Use masking tape to hold it.

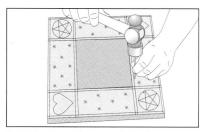

9 Following the traced design, use a nail and hammer to punch holes in the aluminium.

Stencils

Flower design for papier-mâché frame (page 44)

Cut out centre to fit over raised centres

Design for punched metal frame (page 58). Use a photocopier to increase the design to fit the size of the frame.

Tools for making frames

Some of the most useful tools for making frames are shown below. Build up your tool kit gradually—most of the tools can be purchased from your local DIY store.

MITRE SAW Used to cut moulding at an angle to make neatly fitting corners on a frame

FRAMING CLAMP Adjustable clamp that holds the glued frame together

BRAD DRIVER Can be used instead of a pin hammer to nail pins into the back of the frame

CRAFT KNIFE For cutting stencils and other general cutting

PIN HAMMER For hammering panel pins and tacks

GLASS CUTTER Scores the glass before breaking it

MOUNT CUTTER Cuts bevelled edges in mount boards

NAIL PUNCH Recesses nails prior to filling

SHARPENING STONE Smooths the edges of glass after it has been cut

G-CRAMP Adjustable cramp to hold wood together while it is nailed or glued

Index